MOTOWN

T0081931

Ukulele by Chris Kringel
Tracking, mixing, and mastering by Jake Johnson and Chris Kringel

ISBN 978-1-61780-717-6

HAL•LEONARD®
CORPORATION
7777 W. BLUEMOUND RD. P.O. BOX 13819 MILWAUKEE, WI 53213

In Australia Contact:
Hal Leonard Australia Pty. Ltd.
4 Lentara Court
Cheltenham, Victoria, 3192 Australia
Email: ausadmin@halleonard.com.au

Visit Hal Leonard Online at
www.halleonard.com

CONTENTS

Baby Love

Words and Music by Brian Holland, Edward Holland and Lamont Dozier

First note

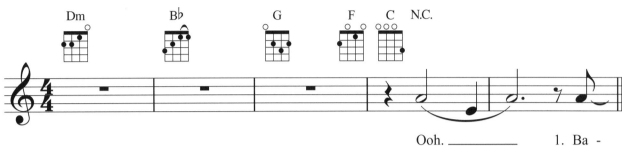

Intro
Moderately fast ♩ = 137

Ooh. _____ 1. Ba -

Verse

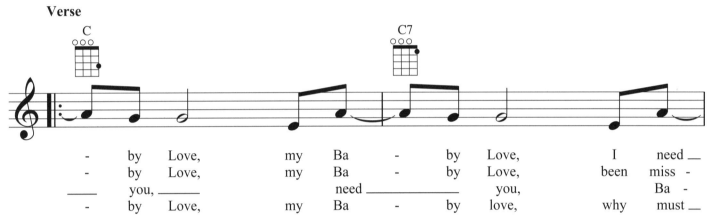

- by Love, my Ba - by Love, I need ___
- by Love, my Ba - by Love, been miss -
___ you, ___ need _____ you, Ba -
- by Love, my Ba - by love, why must ___

___ you, oh, ___ how I need you,
- ing you, miss kiss - ing you.
- by Love, ___ ooh, _____ Ba - by Love.
___ we sep - a - rate, _____ my love?

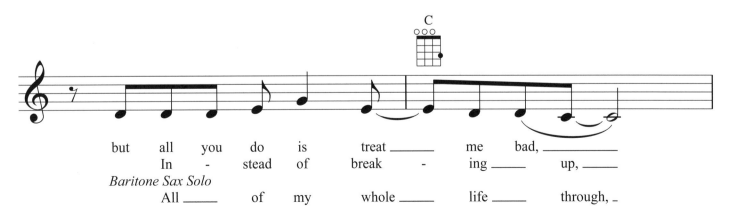

but all you do is treat _____ me bad, _____
In - stead of break - ing _____ up,
Baritone Sax Solo
All _____ of my whole _____ life _____ through, _

F6

C

rip my heart and leave _____ me sad. _____
let's do some kiss - ing and mak - ing up. _____
I nev - er loved no one _____ but you. _____

F6

C

Tell me, what did I _____ do wrong _____ to
Don't ___ throw our love _____ a - way; _____
Why you do me like _____ you do? _____ I

1., 2., 3.

4.

F   C   Dm7   G   Dm7   G

make you stay a - way so long? 2.'Cause Ba -
in my arms why don't you stay? ___ 3. Need ___
get this need. ___   *Solo ends* 4. Ba -
Ooh, ___

D♭

D♭7

3

_____ ooh. _____ 5. Need to

Verse

D♭

D♭7

3   3   3

hold you _____ once a - gain, my love, feel your
___ my love. 6. My Ba - by Love, I need ___
hurt - ing me, till it's hurt - ing me.

5

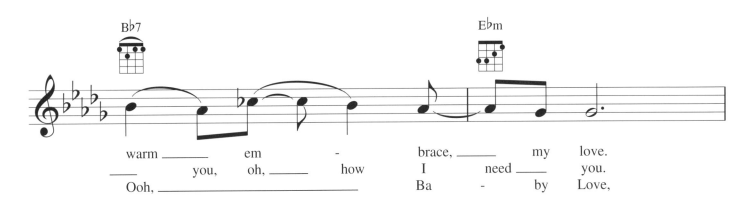

warm _____ em - brace, _____ my love.
____ you, oh, _____ how I need _____ you.
Ooh, _____ Ba - by Love,

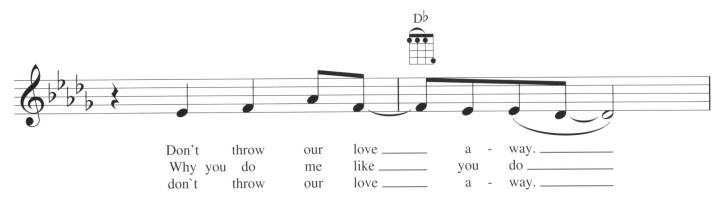

Don't throw our love _____ a - way. _____
Why you do me like _____ you do _____
don`t throw our love _____ a - way. _____

3rd time, fade out

Please don't do me _____ this way. _____
af - ter I've been true _____ to you? _____
Don't throw our love _____ a - way.

Not hap - py like I used to be.
So deep ____ in love _____ with you,

Play 3 times and fade

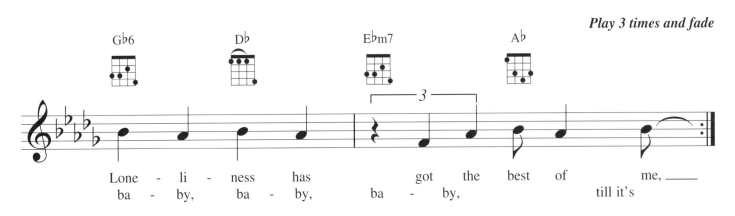

Lone - li - ness has got the best of me, _____
ba - by, ba - by, ba - by, till it's

Easy

Words and Music by Lionel Richie

First note

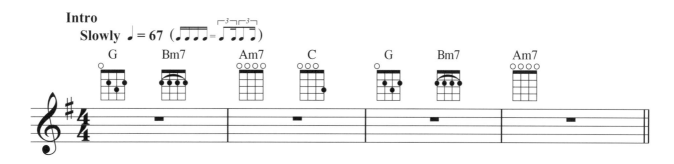

Verse

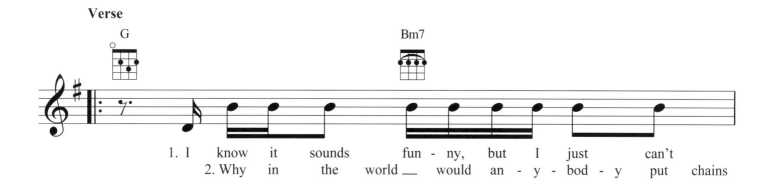

1. I know it sounds fun - ny, but I just can't
2. Why in the world would an - y - bod - y put chains

stand the pain. ___ Girl, I'm leav - ing you ___ to - mor - row. ___
on ___ me? ___ I've paid ___ my dues to make it. ___

Seems to me, ___ girl, you know I've done all ___
Ev - 'ry - bod - y wants - me to be ___ what they want ___

_____ I can; you see, I've begged, stole, _____ and I've bor -
_____ me to be. _____ I'm not hap - py when I try _____ to fake _

- rowed, _____ yeah. _____ }
_____ it, _____ no. _____ } Ooh, _____ that's why I'm eas -

Chorus

- y, I'm eas - y like Sun - day morn - ing. _____

That's why I'm eas - y, _____

_____ I'm eas - y like Sun - day morn -

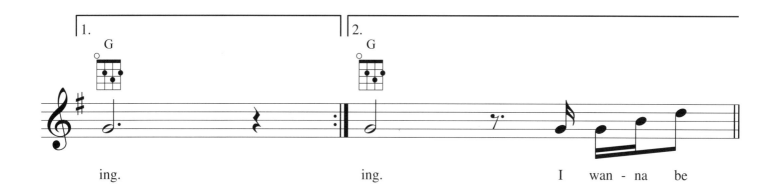

ing.   ing.   I wan - na be

Bridge

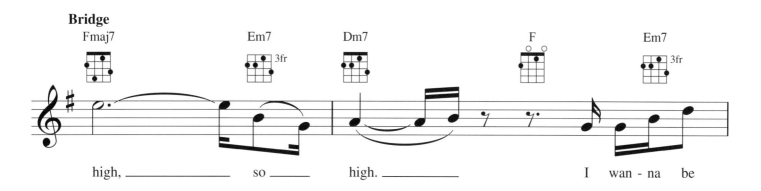

high, _____ so _____ high. _____ I wan - na be

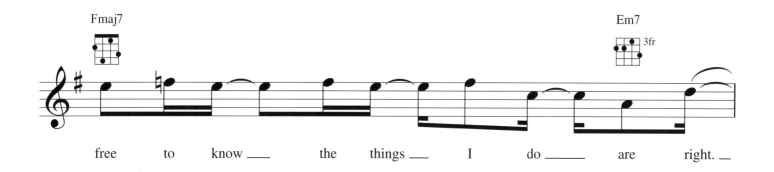

free to know ___ the things ___ I do _____ are right. __

_____ I wan-na be free, ___   just ___

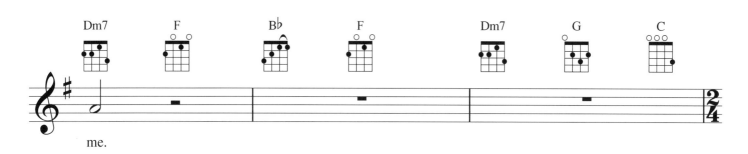

me.

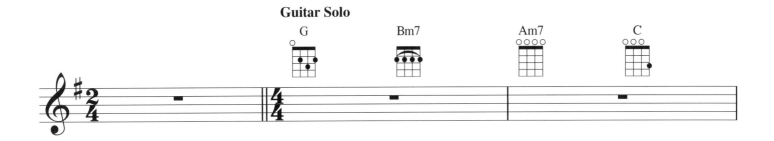

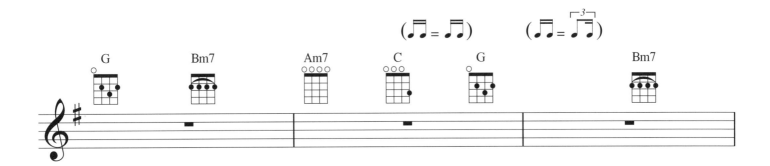

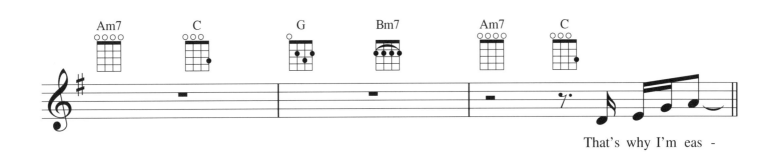

That's why I'm eas -

Chorus

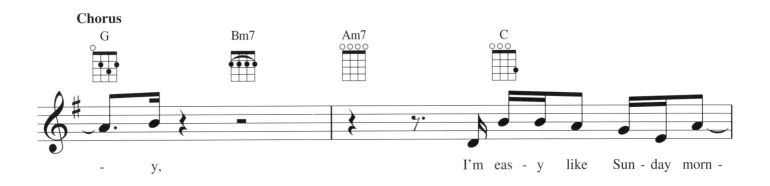

\- y,   I'm eas - y   like   Sun - day morn -

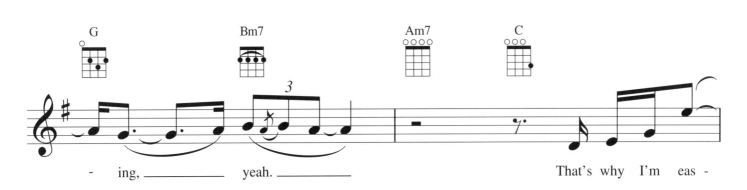

\- ing, _____ yeah. _____   That's why I'm eas -

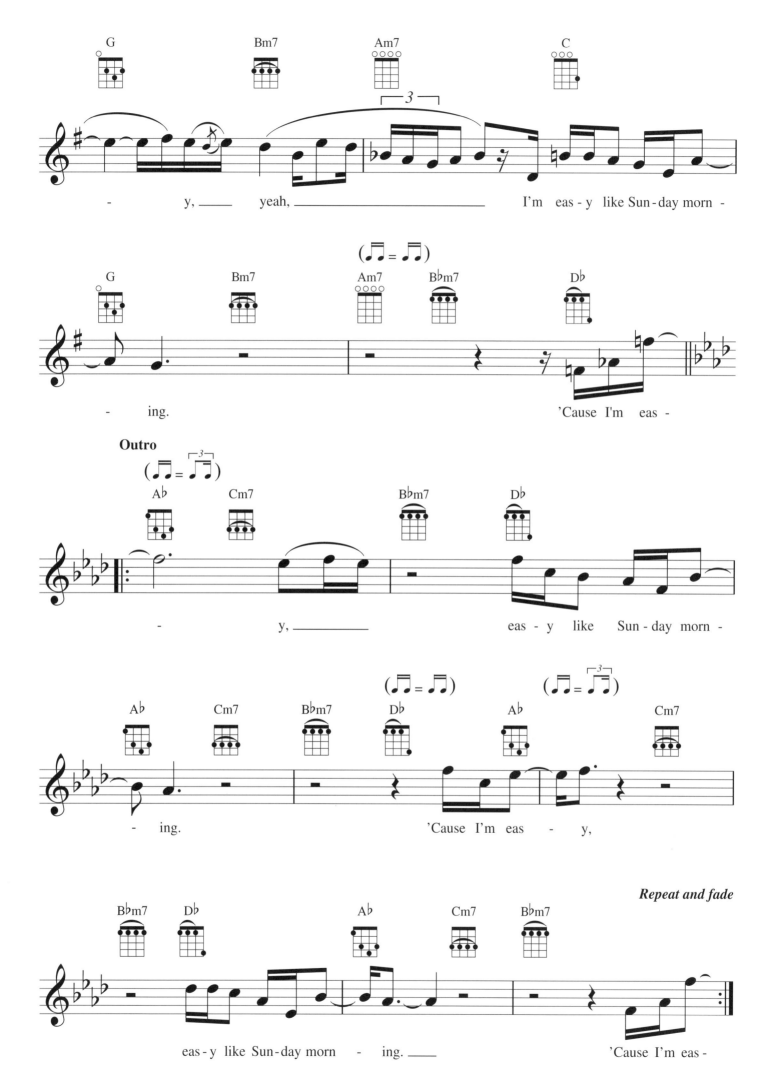

How Sweet It Is
(To Be Loved by You)

Words and Music by Edward Holland, Lamont Dozier and Brian Holland

TRACK 5

First note

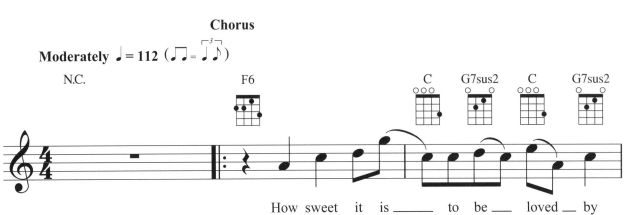

How sweet it is ___ to be ___ loved ___ by

1.
you. ___   Yes,   ba - by.

2.
you. ___   Ooh, ___   ba - by.

Verse
1. I need - ed the ___ shel - ter   of some - one's arms, ___
2. Close ___ my   eyes ___ at night, ___

and there ___ you were. ___
and won - der what would I be with-out ___ you in my ___ life.

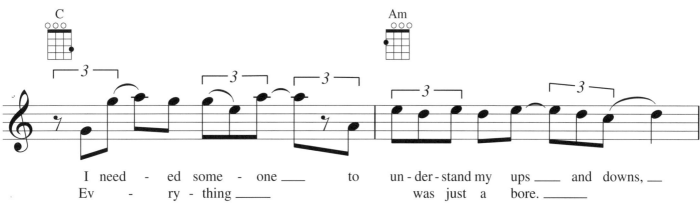

I need - ed some - one ___ to un - der - stand my ups ___ and downs, ___
Ev - ry - thing ___ was just a bore. ___

and there ___ you were. ___
All the things I did, seems I've done 'em be - fore.

With ___ sweet love ___ and de - vo - tion,
But you bright - ened up ___ all ___ my days ___

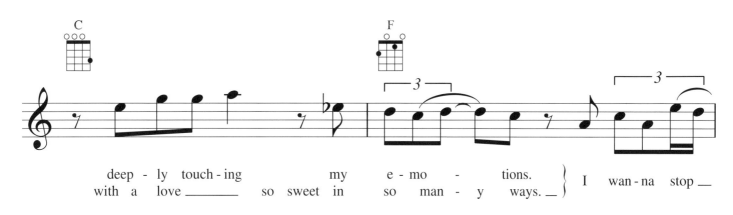

deep - ly touch - ing my e - mo - tions. } I wan - na stop ___
with a love ___ so sweet in so man - y ways. ___ }

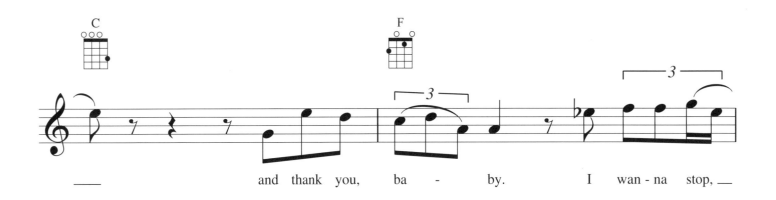

and thank you, ba - by. I wan - na stop, ____

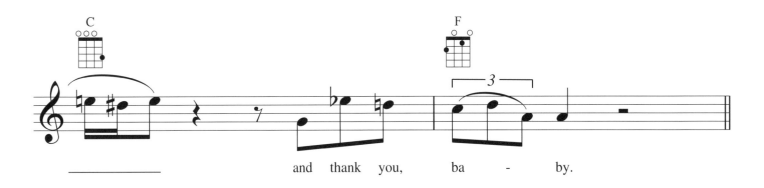

_____ and thank you, ba - by.

Chorus

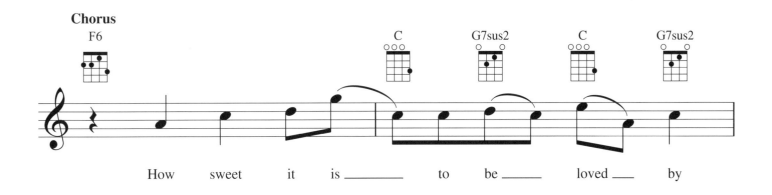

How sweet it is ____ to be ____ loved ____ by

you. ____ Yes, it is, ba - by.

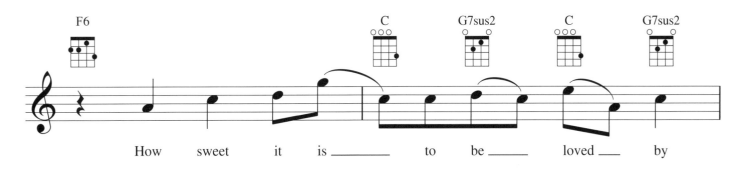

How sweet it is ____ to be ____ loved ____ by

you. _____ Ooh, _ ba - by.

Interlude

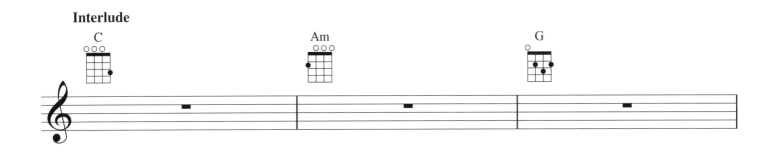

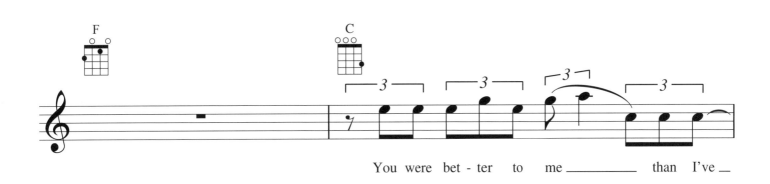

You were bet - ter to me _____ than I've _

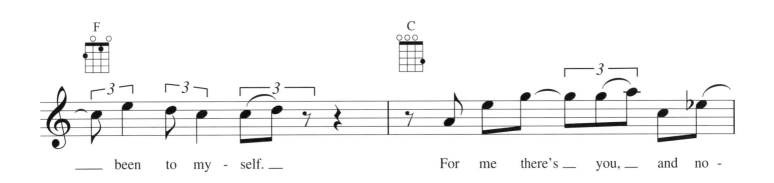

_ been to my - self. _ For me there's _ you, _ and no -

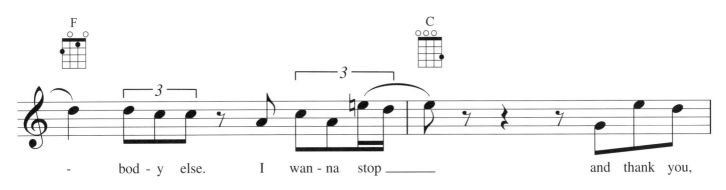

- bod - y else. I wan - na stop _____ and thank you,

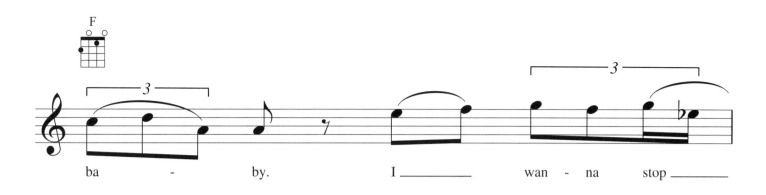

ba - by.   I   wan - na   stop

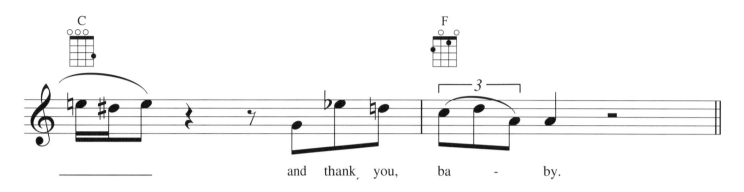

and thank you,   ba -   by.

Chorus

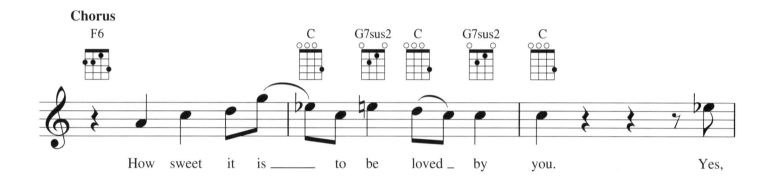

How sweet it is   to be loved   by   you.   Yes,

Begin fade

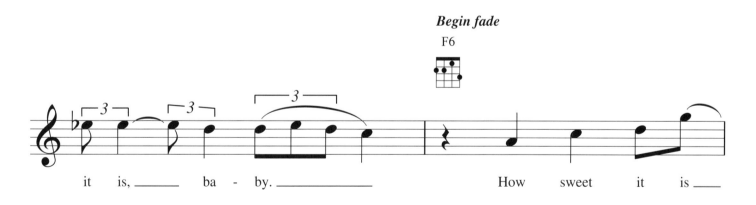

it is,   ba - by.   How sweet it is

Fade out

to be   loved   by   you.

You Can't Hurry Love

Words and Music by Edward Holland, Lamont Dozier and Brian Holland

TRACK 15

First note

Intro
Moderately ♩ = 96

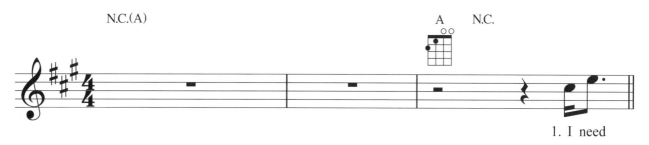

1. I need

Verse

love, love _____ to ease ___ my mind. I need to

find, find ___ some-one to call ___ mine, but ma - ma said, ___ "You

Chorus

can't hur - ry love. ___ No, you just have to wait." ___ She said,
"Can't hur - ry love. ___ No, you just have to wait." ___ She said,

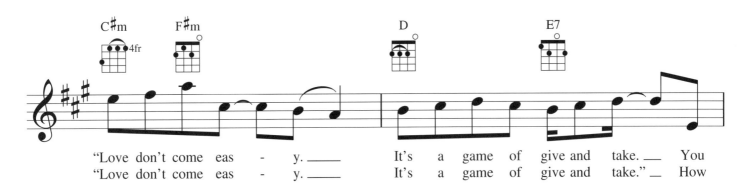

"Love don't come eas - y. _____   It's   a   game of give and take. __ You
"Love don't come eas - y. _____   It's   a   game of give and take." __ How

can't   hur - ry   love. __   No,   you   just have   to   wait. __   You got - ta
long must   I   wait, __ how much more can I   take _____   be - fore ___

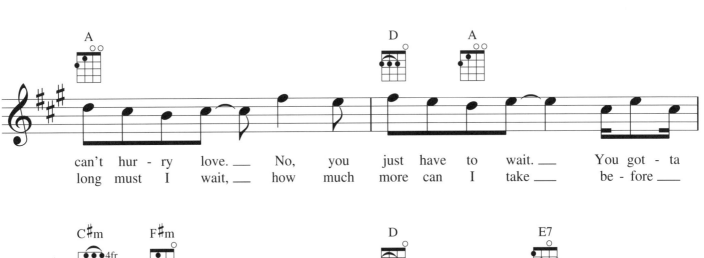

trust, _____ give   it   time,   no   mat - ter how   long __ it   takes." But
lone - li - ness _____   will   cause my heart, heart __ to break? No,

Bridge

how man - y heart-aches must I   stand _____   be - fore   I   find _
I   can't bear __   to   live   my   life a - lone.   I   grow im -

_____ a   love _____   to   let   me   love a - gain? __   Right now the
pa - tient for _____   a   love   to   call my own, __   but when I

18

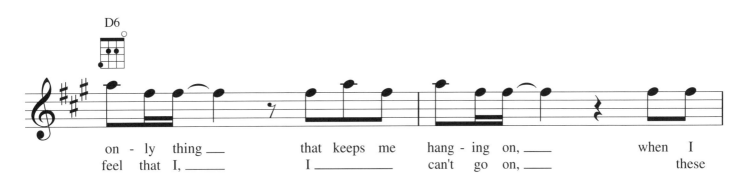

on - ly thing ___   that keeps me   hang - ing on, ___   when I
feel that I, ___   I ___ can't go on, ___   these

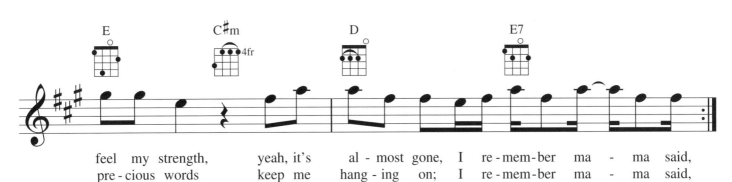

feel my strength,   yeah, it's   al - most gone, I re - mem - ber ma - ma said,
pre - cious words   keep me   hang - ing on; I re - mem - ber ma - ma said,

Chorus

"Can't hur - ry   love. ___   No,   you   just have   to wait."   She said,
can't hur - ry   love. ___   No,   you   just have   to wait."   She said,

1.

"Love don't come eas - y, ___   it's a game of give and take. ___ You
"Trust, ___ give it time, no

2.

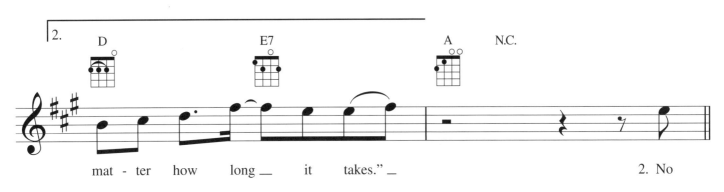

mat - ter how   long ___ it takes." ___   2. No

Verse

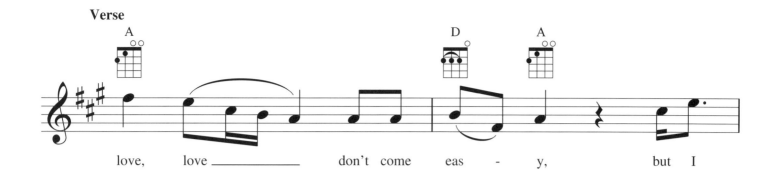

love, love _____ don't come eas - y, but I

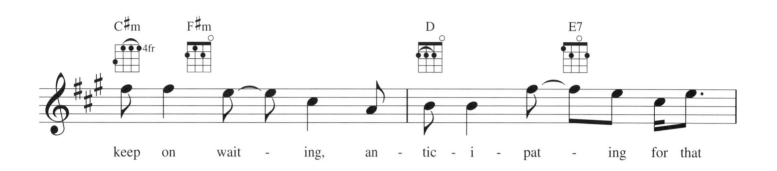

keep on wait - ing, an - tic - i - pat - ing for that

soft voice to talk to me at night, ___ for some

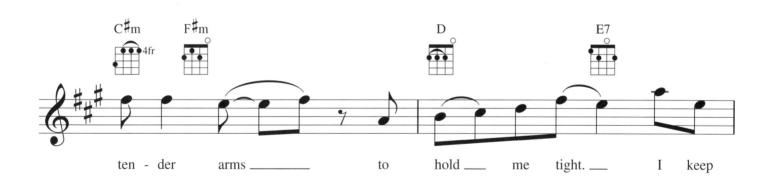

ten - der arms _____ to hold ___ me tight. ___ I keep

wait - ing. I keep on wait - ing. ___ But it ain't

20

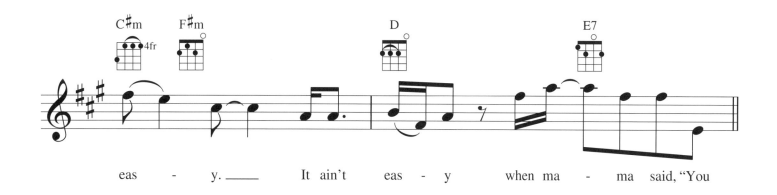

eas - y. ____ It ain't eas - y when ma - ma said, "You

Chorus

can't hur - ry love. ____ No, you just have to wait." She said,

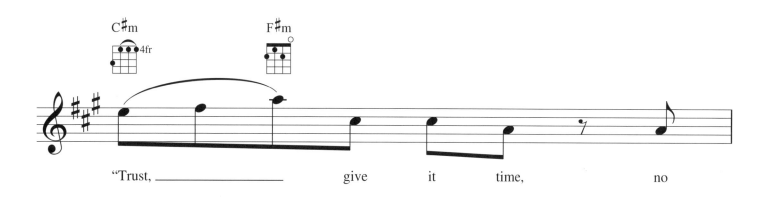

"Trust, _____ give it time, no

Begin fade

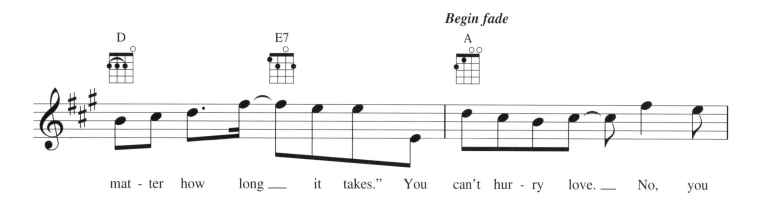

mat - ter how long ___ it takes." You can't hur - ry love. ___ No, you

Fade out

just have to wait. She said, "Love don't come eas - y." ____

I Heard It Through the Grapevine

Words and Music by Norman J. Whitfield and Barrett Strong

TRACK 7

First note

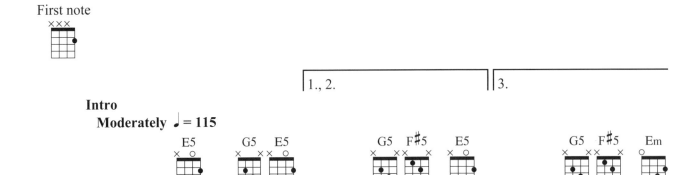

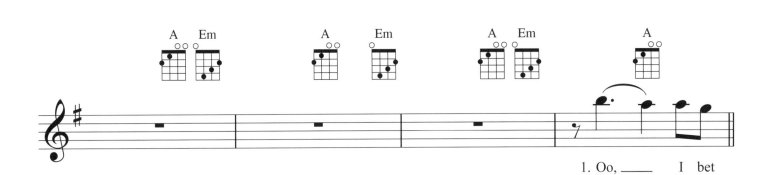

Intro
Moderately ♩ = 115

1., 2.   3.

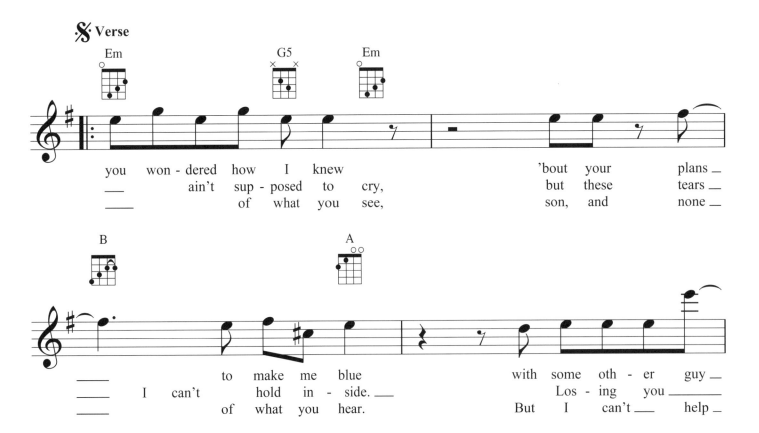

1. Oo, ____ I bet

Verse

Em   G5   Em

you   won - dered how   I   knew   'bout   your   plans ____
____   ain't   sup - posed   to   cry,   but   these   tears ____
____   of   what   you   see,   son,   and   none ____

B   A

____   to   make   me   blue   with   some   oth - er   guy ____
____   I   can't   hold   in - side. ____   Los - ing   you ____
____   of   what   you   hear.   But   I   can't ____ help ____

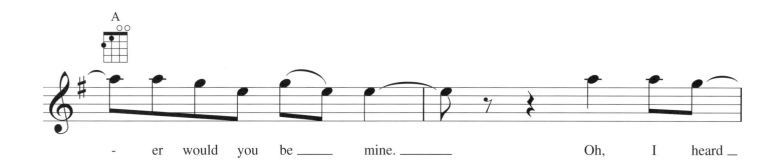

-er would you be ____ mine. _____ Oh, I heard ___

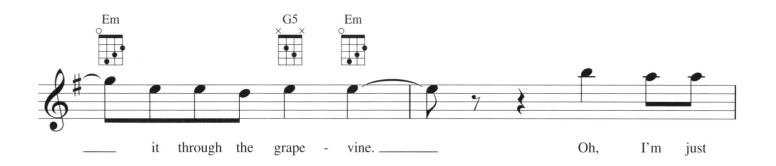

____ it through the grape - vine. _____ Oh, I'm just

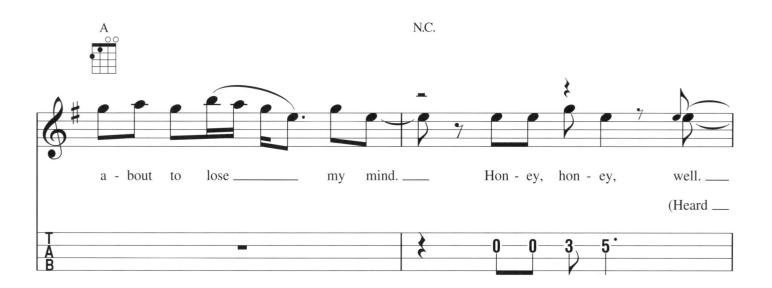

a - bout to lose _____ my mind. ____ Hon - ey, hon - ey, well. ____

(Heard ___

5th time, To Coda

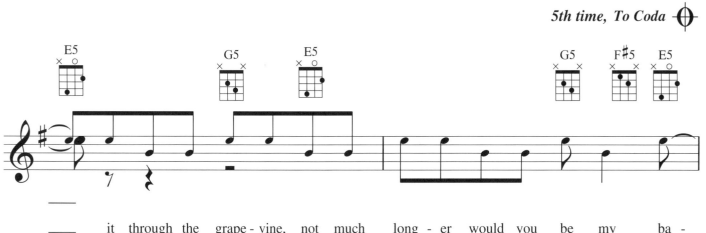

____ it through the grape - vine, not much long - er would you be my ba -

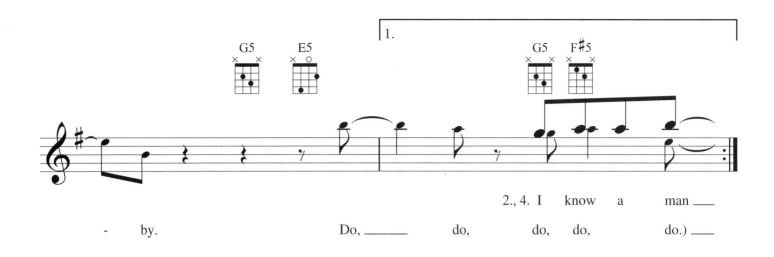

2., 4. I know a man ___

\- by.   Do, _____ do,   do,   do,   do.) ___

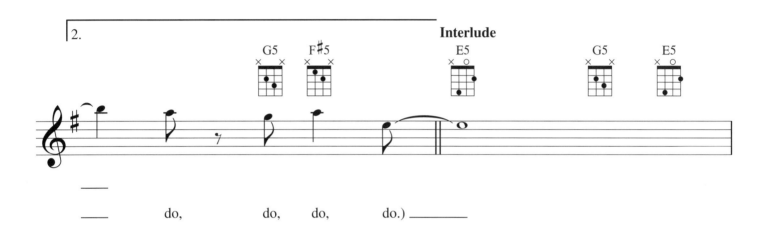

___

___ do,   do,   do,   do.) _____

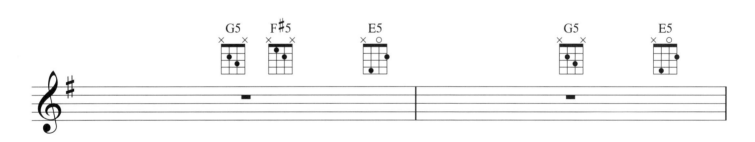

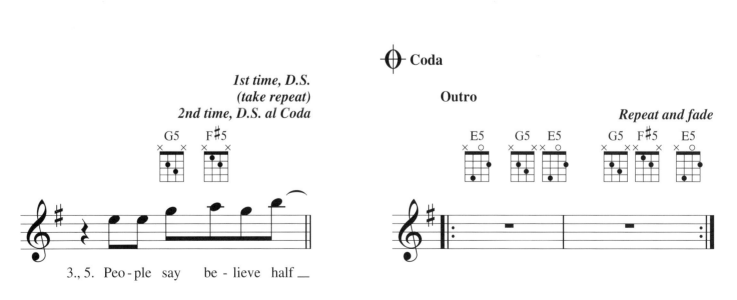

1st time, D.S.
(take repeat)
2nd time, D.S. al Coda

Outro

Repeat and fade

3., 5. Peo - ple say   be - lieve half ___

I Want You Back

Words and Music by Freddie Perren, Alphonso Mizell, Berry Gordy and Deke Richards

TRACK 9

First note

Intro
Moderate Soul ♩ = 100

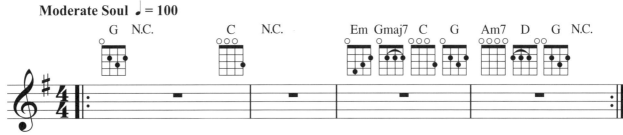

w/ Voc. ad lib.

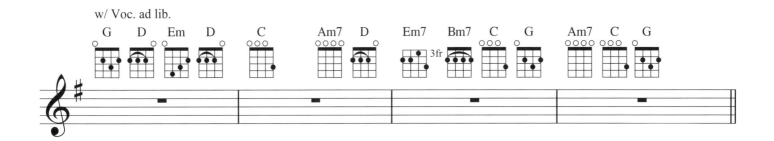

𝄋 Verse

1. When I had ___ you to ___ my-self, ___ I did-n't want you a-round. ___ Those
2. Try-ing to live with-out ___ your love ___ is one ___ long sleep-less night. _____

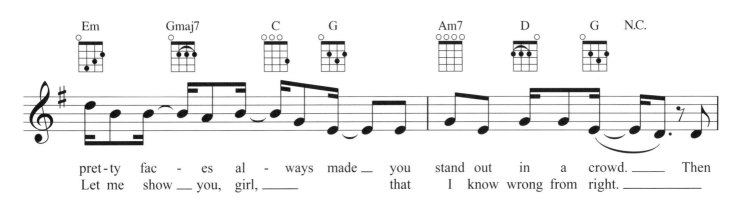

pret-ty fac-es al-ways made ___ you stand out in a crowd. _____ Then
Let me show ___ you, girl, _____ that I know wrong from right. _____

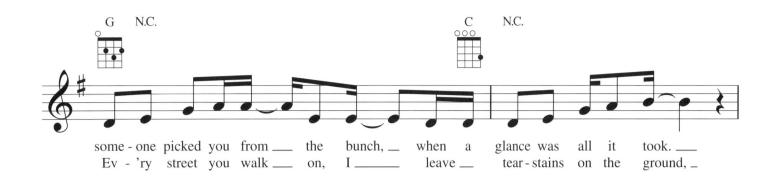

some - one picked you from ___ the bunch, ___ when a glance was all it took. ___
Ev - 'ry street you walk ___ on, I _____ leave ___ tear - stains on the ground, __

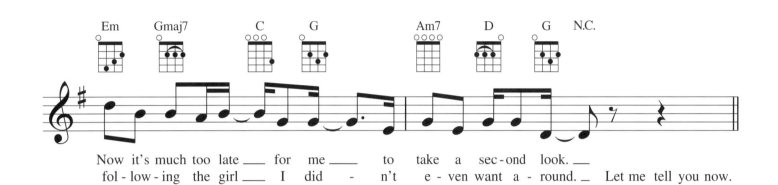

Now it's much too late ___ for me ___ to take a sec - ond look. ___
fol - low - ing the girl ___ I did - n't e - ven want a - round. _ Let me tell you now.

Chorus

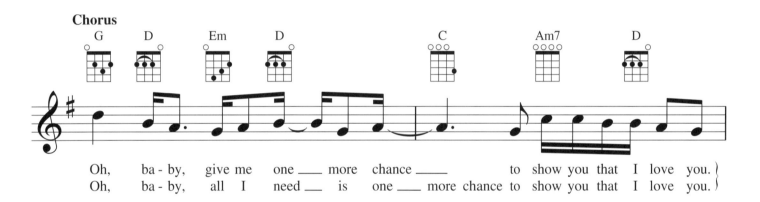

Oh, ba - by, give me one ___ more chance _____ to show you that I love you.
Oh, ba - by, all I need ___ is one ___ more chance to show you that I love you.

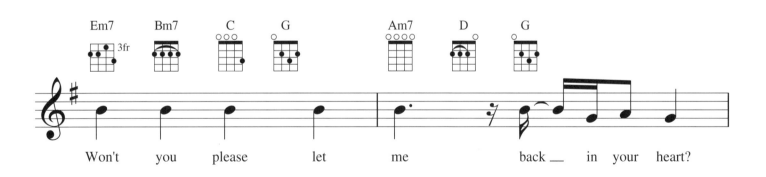

Won't you please let me back ___ in your heart?

To Coda ⊕

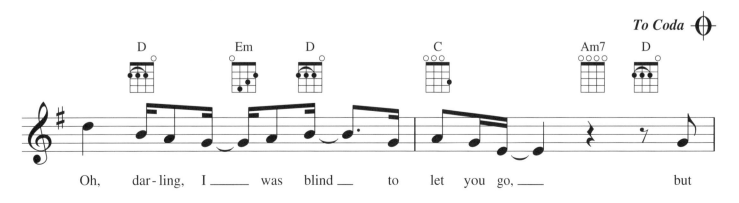

Oh, dar - ling, I _____ was blind ___ to let you go, ___ but

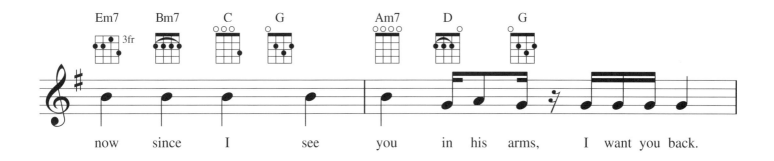

now   since   I   see   you   in   his   arms,   I   want   you   back.

Oh,   I   do   now.   I   want you back,   ooh,   ooh,   ba - by,   I   want you back.

D.S. al Coda

Yeah,   yeah,   yeah, ___   I   want   you   back.   Na,   na,   na,   na.

⊕ Coda

Bridge

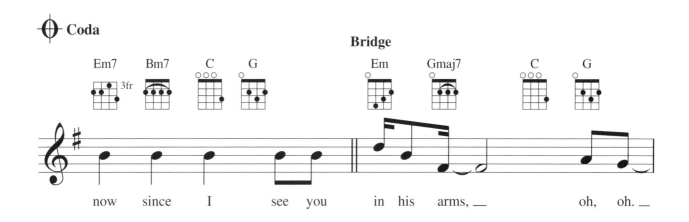

now   since   I   see   you   in   his   arms, ___   oh,   oh. ___

w/ Voc. ad lib.

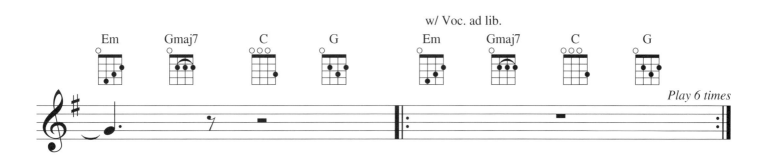

Play 6 times

___

Chorus

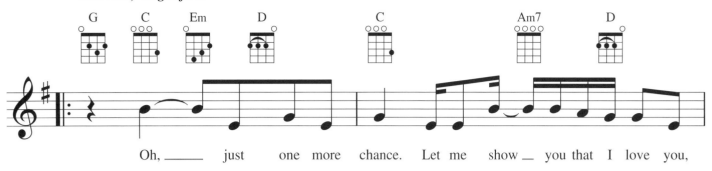

Oh, _____ just one more chance. Let me show _ you that I love you,

ba - by, ba - by, ba - by. _____ For - get what hap - pened then. _

2nd time, Fade out

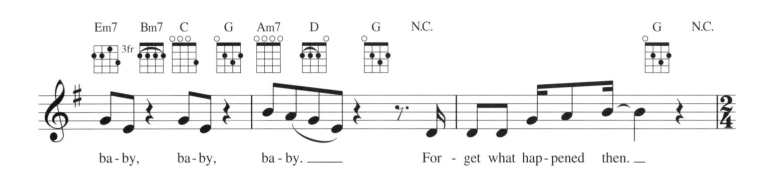

Let me live a - gain. _____ Oh, ba - by, I was blind _ to let _

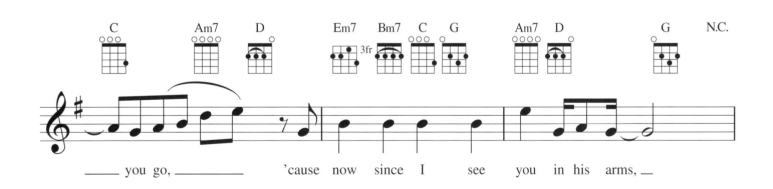

_____ you go, _____ _____ 'cause now since I see you in his arms, _

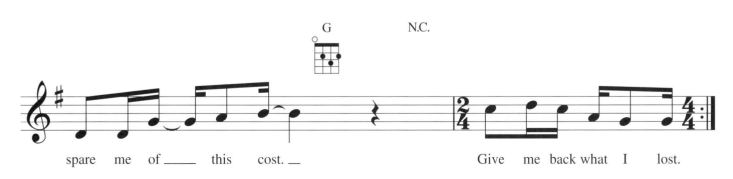

spare me of _____ this cost. _ Give me back what I lost.

TRACK 11

My Cherie Amour

Words and Music by Stevie Wonder, Sylvia Moy and Henry Cosby

First note

Intro
Moderately ♩ = 130

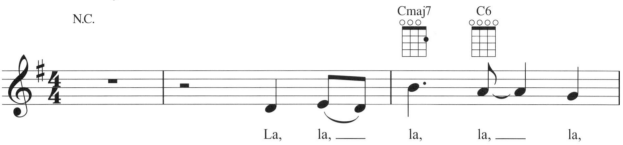

La, la, ____ la, la, ____ la,

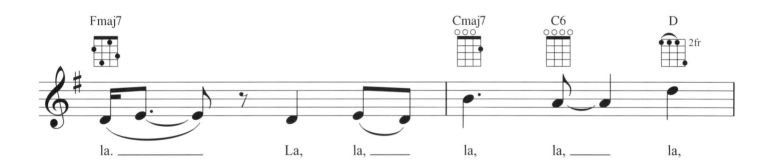

la. ____ La, la, la, la, ____ la,

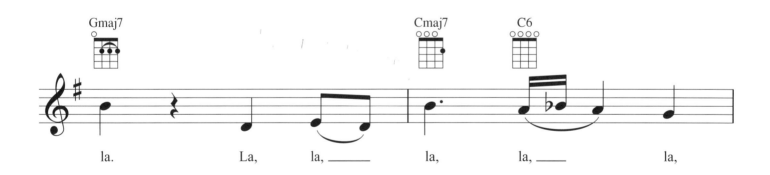

la. La, la, ____ la, la, ____ la,

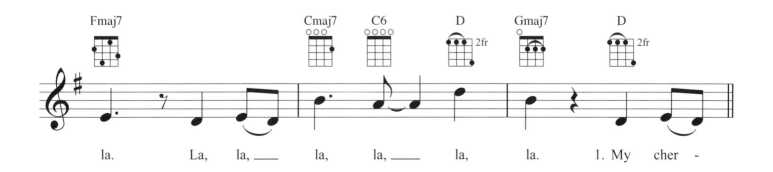

la. La, la, ____ la, la, ____ la, la. 1. My cher -

Verse

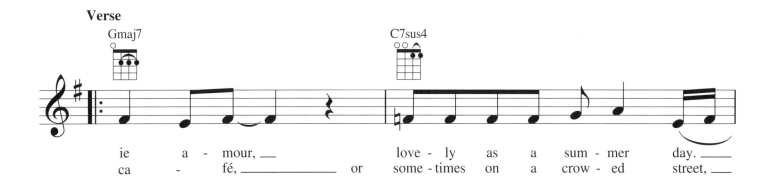

ie a - mour, _____ love - ly as a sum - mer day. _____
ca - fé, _____ or some - times on a crow - ed street, _____

_____
_____ I've _____ been _ near _____ you, _____ but you
My cher - ie a - mour, _

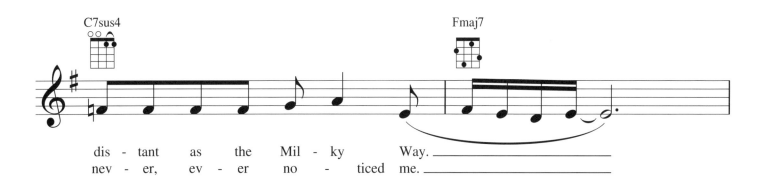

dis - tant as the Mil - ky Way. _____
nev - er, ev - er no - ticed me. _____

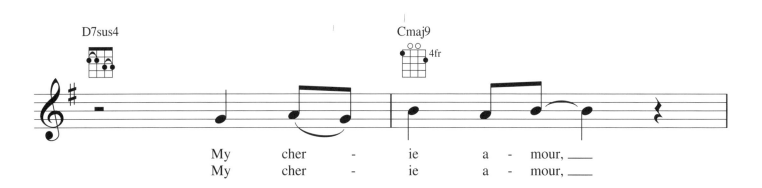

My cher - ie a - mour, _____
My cher - ie a - mour, _____

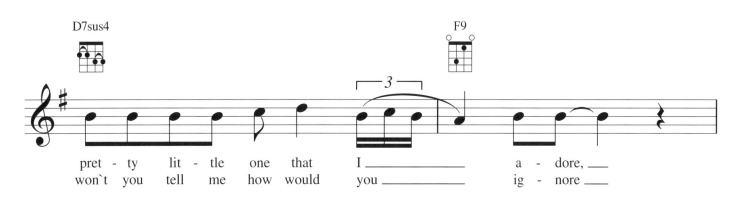

pret - ty lit - tle one that I _____ a - dore, _____
won`t you tell me how would you _____ ig - nore _____

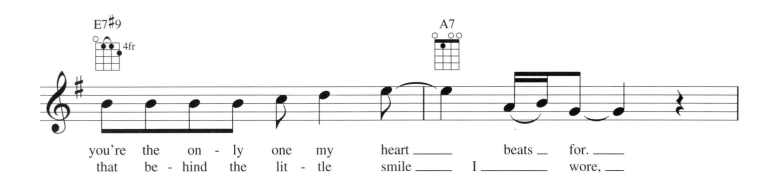

you're the on - ly one my heart _____ beats _ for. _____
that be - hind the lit - tle smile _____ I _____ wore, ___

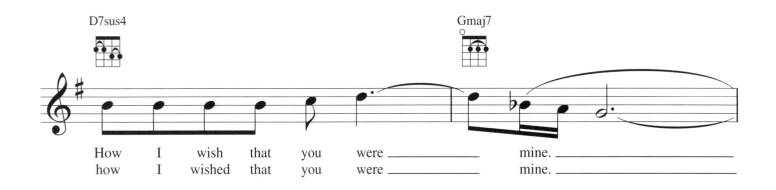

How I wish that you were _____ mine. _____
how I wished that you were _____ mine. _____

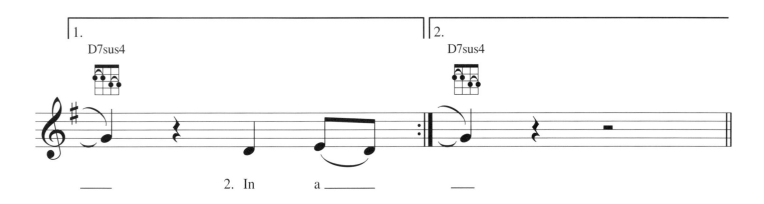

1.

2.

____ 2. In a _____ ___

Interlude

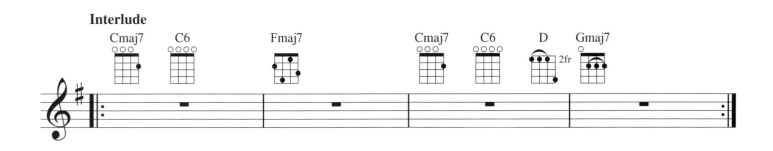

Cmaj7   C6   Fmaj7   Cmaj7   C6   D   Gmaj7

Bridge

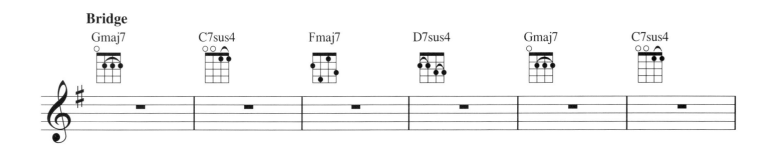

Gmaj7   C7sus4   Fmaj7   D7sus4   Gmaj7   C7sus4

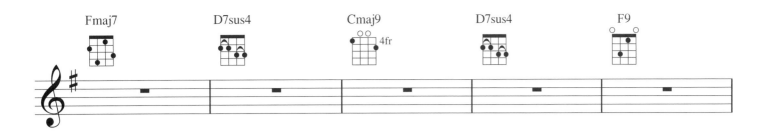

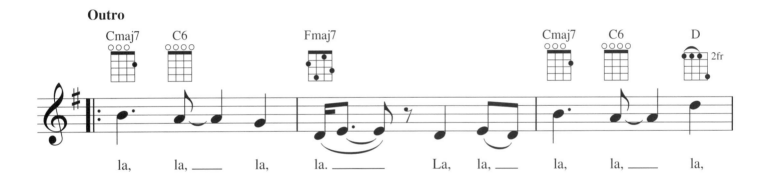

La, la, ___

Outro

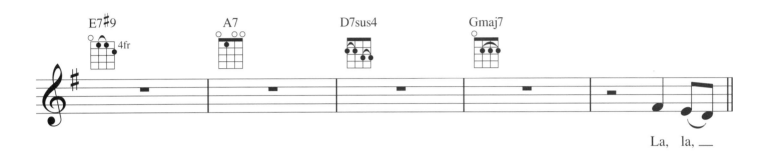

la,   la, ____ la,   la. _____ La,   la, ____ la,   la, ____ la,

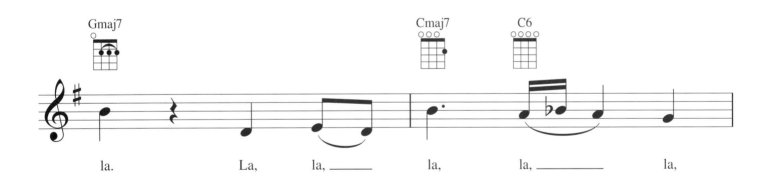

la.   La,   la, _____ la,   la, _____ la,

Repeat and fade

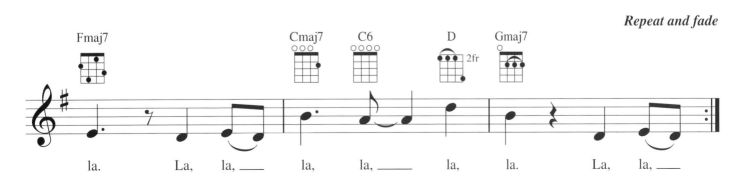

la.   La,   la, ____ la,   la, ____ la,   la.   La,   la, ____

TRACK 13

My Girl

Words and Music by William "Smokey" Robinson and Ronald White

First note

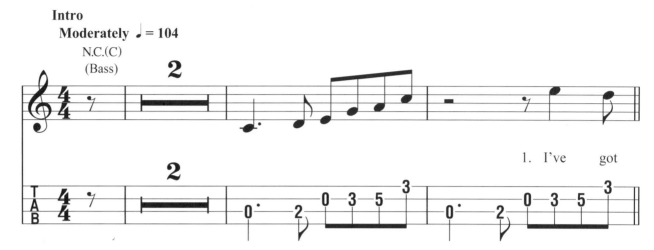

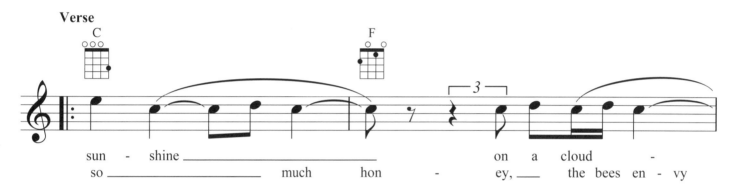

Chorus

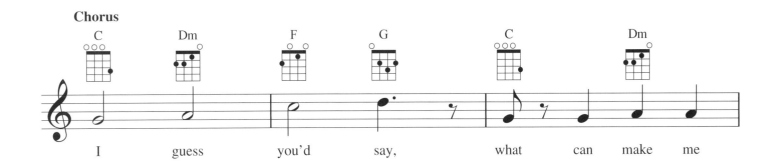

I guess you'd say, what can make me

feel this way? _____ My girl, (my girl,) (my girl,) talk - in' 'bout _____

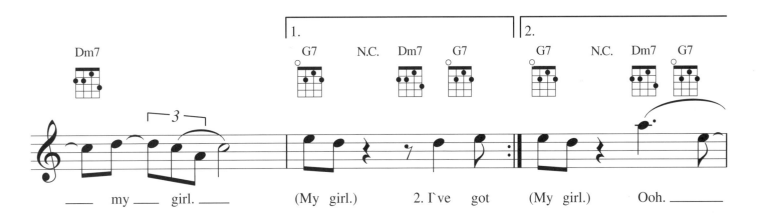

_____ my _____ girl. _____ (My girl.) 2. I've got (My girl.) Ooh. _____

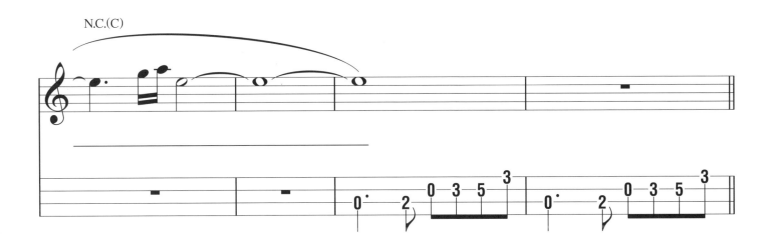

Interlude

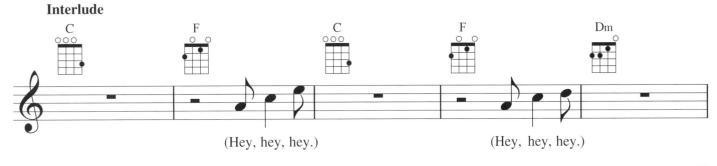

(Hey, hey, hey.)   (Hey, hey, hey.)

35

Ooh, _____ yeah. _____ 3. I don't

Verse

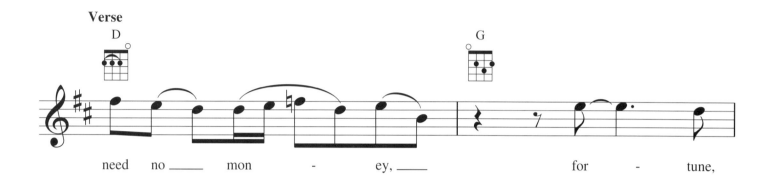

need no _____ mon - ey, _____ for - tune,

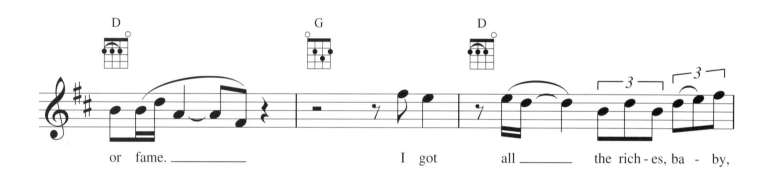

or fame. _____ I got all _____ the rich - es, ba - by,

one man _____ can claim. _____ Well, ___

Chorus

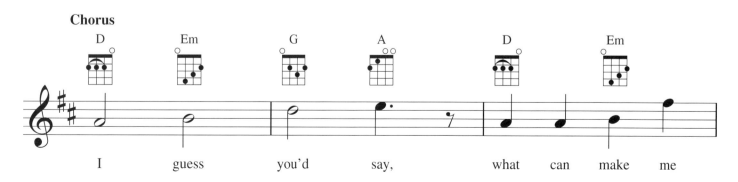

I guess you'd say, what can make me

feel ___ this way? _____ My girl, (my girl,) (my girl,) talk - in' 'bout __

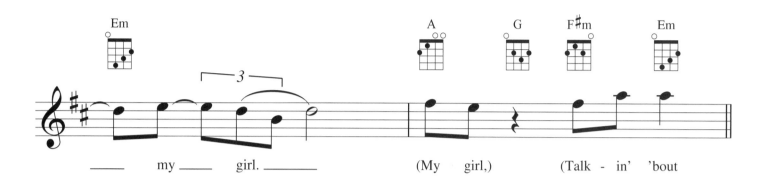

___ my ___ girl. _____ (My girl,) (Talk - in' 'bout

Outro

my girl.) I got sun - shine on a cloud - y day _____ with my __

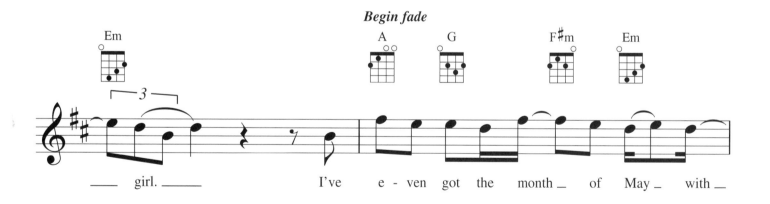

___ girl. _____ I've e - ven got the month __ of May _ with __

___ my girl. _____ Talk - in' 'bout. __

HAL·LEONARD UKULELE PLAY-ALONG

Now you can play your favorite songs on your uke with great-sounding backing tracks to help you sound like a bona fide pro!

1. POP HITS
American Pie • Copacabana (At the Copa) • Crocodile Rock • Kokomo • Lean on Me • Stand by Me • Twist and Shout • What the World Needs Now Is Love.
00701451 Book/CD Pack.............$14.99

2. UKE CLASSICS
Ain't She Sweet • Five Foot Two, Eyes of Blue (Has Anybody Seen My Girl?) • It's Only a Paper Moon • Living in the Sunlight, Loving in the Moonlight • Pennies from Heaven • Tonight You Belong to Me • Ukulele Lady • When I'm Cleaning Windows.
00701452 Book/CD Pack.............$12.99

3. HAWAIIAN FAVORITES
Aloha Oe • Blue Hawaii • Harbor Lights • The Hawaiian Wedding Song (Ke Kali Nei Au) • Mele Kalikimaka • Sleepy Lagoon • Sweet Someone • Tiny Bubbles.
00701453 Book/CD Pack.............$12.99

4. CHILDREN'S SONGS
Do-Re-Mi • The Hokey Pokey • It's a Small World • My Favorite Things • Puff the Magic Dragon • Sesame Street Theme • Splish Splash • This Land Is Your Land.
00701454 Book/CD Pack.............$12.99

5. CHRISTMAS SONGS [INCLUDES TAB]
Do You Hear What I Hear • Feliz Navidad • Frosty the Snow Man • Here Comes Santa Claus (Right down Santa Claus Lane) • Jingle-Bell Rock • Nuttin' for Christmas • Rudolph the Red-Nosed Reindeer • Santa Claus Is Comin' to Town.
00701696 Book/CD Pack.............$12.99

6. LENNON & McCARTNEY
And I Love Her • Day Tripper • Here, There and Everywhere • Hey Jude • Let It Be • Norwegian Wood (This Bird Has Flown) • Nowhere Man • Yesterday.
00701723 Book/CD Pack.............$12.99

7. DISNEY FAVORITES
Alice in Wonderland • The Bare Necessities • Candle on the Water • Chim Chim Cher-ee • A Dream Is a Wish Your Heart Makes • Mickey Mouse March • Supercalifragilisticexpialidocious • Under the Sea.
00701724 Book/CD Pack.............$12.99

8. CHART HITS
All the Right Moves • Bubbly • Hey, Soul Sister • I'm Yours • Toes • Use Somebody • Viva la Vida • You're Beautiful.
00701745 Book/CD Pack.............$12.99

9. THE SOUND OF MUSIC
Climb Ev'ry Mountain • Do-Re-Mi • Edelweiss • Maria • My Favorite Things • Sixteen Going on Seventeen • Something Good • The Sound of Music.
00701784 Book/CD Pack.............$12.99

11. CHRISTMAS STRUMMING
Away in a Manger • Deck the Hall • The First Noel • Hark! the Herald Angels Sing • Jingle Bells • Joy to the World • O Come, All Ye Faithful (Adeste Fideles) • We Three Kings of Orient Are.
00702458 Book/CD Pack.............$12.99

13. UKULELE SONGS
Daughter • Dream a Little Dream of Me • Elderly Woman Behind the Counter in a Small Town • Last Kiss • More Than You Know • Sleepless Nights • Tonight You Belong to Me • Yellow Ledbetter.
00702599 Book/CD Pack.............$12.99

FOR MORE INFORMATION, SEE YOUR LOCAL MUSIC DEALER, OR WRITE TO:

HAL·LEONARD® CORPORATION
7777 W. BLUEMOUND RD. P.O. BOX 13819 MILWAUKEE, WI 53213

www.halleonard.com
Prices, contents, and availability subject to change without notice.
Disney characters and artwork © Disney Enterprises, Inc.

1111

Learn to play the
Ukulele
with these great Hal Leonard books!

Hal Leonard Ukulele Method Book 1
by Lil' Rev

The *Hal Leonard Ukulele Method* is designed for anyone just learning to play ukulele. This comprehensive and easy-to-use beginner's guide by acclaimed performer and uke master Lil' Rev includes many fun songs of different styles to learn and play. The accompanying CD contains 46 tracks of songs for demonstration and play along. Includes: types of ukuleles, tuning, music reading, melody playing, chords, strumming, scales, tremolo, music notation and tablature, a variety of music styles, ukulele history and much more.

00695847 Book Only.. $5.99
00695832 Book/CD Pack $10.99
00320534 DVD $14.95

Hal Leonard Ukulele Method Book 2
by Lil' Rev

Book 2 picks up where Book 1 left off, featuring more fun songs and examples to strengthen skills and make practicing more enjoyable. Topics include lessons on chord families, hammer-ons, pull-offs, and slides, 6/8 time, ukulele history, and much more. The accompanying CD contains 51 tracks of songs for demonstration and play along.

00695948 Book Only.. $5.95
00695949 Book/CD Pack $9.95

Hal Leonard Ukulele Chord Finder
Easy-to-Use Guide to Over 1,000 Ukulele Chords

Learn to play chords on the ukulele with this comprehensive, yet easy-to-use book. *The Ukulele Chord Finder* contains more than a thousand chord diagrams for the most important 28 chord types, including three voicings for each chord. Also includes a lesson on chord construction and a fingerboard chart of the ukulele neck!

00695803 9" x 12".. $6.95
00695902 6" x 9".. $4.99

Hal Leonard Ukulele Scale Finder
by Chad Johnson
Easy-to-Use Guide to Over 1,300 Ukulele Scales

Learn to play scales on the ukulele with this comprehensive yet easy-to-use book. *The Ukulele Scale Finder* contains over 1,300 scale diagrams for the most often-used scales and modes, including multiple patterns for each scale. Also includes a lesson on scale construction and a fingerboard chart of the ukulele neck!

00696378 9" x 12".. $6.99

Easy Songs for Ukulele
Play the Melodies of 20 Pop, Folk, Country, and Blues Songs
by Lil' Rev

Play along with your favorite tunes from the Beatles, Elvis, Johnny Cash, Woody Guthrie, Simon & Garfunkel, and more! The songs are presented in the order of difficulty, beginning with simple rhythms and melodies and ending with chords and notes up the neck. The audio CD features every song played with guitar accompaniment, so you can hear how each song sounds and then play along when you're ready.

00695904 Book/CD Pack $14.99
00695905 Book.. $6.99

Irving Berlin Songs Arranged for the "Uke"

20 great songs with full instructions, including: Alexander's Ragtime Band • White Christmas • Easter Parade • Say It with Music • and more.

00005558 7" x 10-1/4" $6.95

Fretboard Roadmaps – Ukulele
The Essential Patterns That All the Pros Know and Use
by Fred Sokolow & Jim Beloff

Take your uke playing to the next level! Tunes and exercises in standard notation and tab illustrate each technique. Absolute beginners can follow the diagrams and instruction step-by-step, while intermediate and advanced players can use the chapters non-sequentially to increase their understanding of the ukulele. The CD includes 59 demo and play-along tracks.

00695901 Book/CD Pack.. $14.99

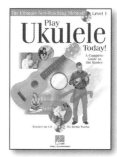

Play Ukulele Today!
A Complete Guide to the Basics
by Barrett Tagliarino

This is the ultimate self-teaching method for ukulele! Includes a CD with full demo tracks and over 60 great songs. You'll learn: care for the instrument; how to produce sound; reading music notation and rhythms; and more.

00699638 Book/CD Pack... $9.99

HAL•LEONARD® CORPORATION

7777 W. BLUEMOUND RD. P.O. BOX 13819
MILWAUKEE, WISCONSIN 53213

www.halleonard.com

Prices, contents and availability subject to change without notice. Prices listed in U.S. funds.

0911

Ride the Ukulele Wave!

The Beach Boys for Ukulele

This folio features 20 favorites, including: Barbara Ann • Be True to Your School • California Girls • Fun, Fun, Fun • God Only Knows • Good Vibrations • Help Me Rhonda • I Get Around • In My Room • Kokomo • Little Deuce Coupe • Sloop John B • Surfin' U.S.A. • Wouldn't It Be Nice • and more!

00701726 . . . . $14.99

Disney Songs for Ukulele

20 great Disney classics arranged for all uke players, including: Beauty and the Beast • Bibbidi-Bobbidi-Boo (The Magic Song) • Can You Feel the Love Tonight • Chim Chim Cher-ee • Heigh-Ho • It's a Small World • Some Day My Prince Will Come • We're All in This Together • When You Wish upon a Star • and more.

00701708 . . . . $12.99

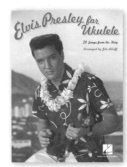

Elvis Presley for Ukulele

arr. Jim Beloff

20 classic hits from The King: All Shook Up • Blue Hawaii • Blue Suede Shoes • Can't Help Falling in Love • Don't • Heartbreak Hotel • Hound Dog • Jailhouse Rock • Love Me • Love Me Tender • Return to Sender • Suspicious Minds • Teddy Bear • and more.

00701004 . . . . $14.99

The Beatles for Ukulele

Ukulele players can strum, sing and pick along with 20 Beatles classics! Includes: All You Need Is Love • Eight Days a Week • Good Day Sunshine • Here, There and Everywhere • Let It Be • Love Me Do • Penny Lane • Yesterday • and more.

00700154 . . . . $16.99

Folk Songs for Ukulele

A great collection to take along to the campfire! 60 folk songs, including: Amazing Grace • Buffalo Gals • Camptown Races • For He's a Jolly Good Fellow • Good Night Ladies • Home on the Range • I've Been Working on the Railroad • Kumbaya • My Bonnie Lies over the Ocean • On Top of Old Smoky • Scarborough Fair • Swing Low, Sweet Chariot • Take Me Out to the Ball Game • Yankee Doodle • and more.

00696068 . . . . $12.99

Hawaiian Songs for Ukulele

Over thirty songs from the state that made the ukulele famous, including: Beyond the Rainbow • Hanalei Moon • Ka-lu-a • Lovely Hula Girl • Mele Kalikimaka • One More Aloha • Sea Breeze • Tiny Bubbles • Waikiki • and more.

00696065 . . . . $9.99

Irving Berlin Songs Arranged for the "Uke"

20 great songs with full instructions, including: Always • Blue Skies • Easter Parade • How Deep Is the Ocean (How High Is the Sky) • A Pretty Girl Is like a Melody • Say It with Music • What'll I Do? • White Christmas • and more.

00005558 . . . . $6.95

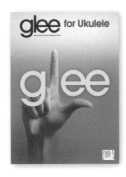

Glee

Music from the Fox Television Show for Ukulele

20 favorites for Gleeks to strum and sing, including: Bad Romance • Beautiful • Defying Gravity • Don't Stop Believin' • No Air • Proud Mary • Rehab • True Colors • and more.

00701722 . . . $14.99

Worship Songs for Ukulele

25 worship songs: Amazing Grace (My Chains are Gone) • Blessed Be Your Name • Enough • God of Wonders • Holy Is the Lord • How Great Is Our God • In Christ Alone • Love the Lord • Mighty to Save • Sing to the King • Step by Step • We Fall Down • and more.

00702546 . . . . $12.99

The Daily Ukulele

compiled and arranged by Liz and Jim Beloff

Strum a different song everyday with easy arrangements of 365 of your favorite songs in one big songbook! Includes favorites by the Beatles, Beach Boys, and Bob Dylan, folk songs, pop songs, kids' songs, Christmas carols, and Broadway and Hollywood tunes, all with a spiral binding for ease of use.

00240356 . . . . $34.99

Jake Shimabukuro – Peace Love Ukulele

Deemed "the Hendrix of the ukulele," Hawaii native Jake Shimabukuro is a uke virtuoso. Our songbook features note-for-note transcriptions with ukulele tablature of Jake's masterful playing on all the CD tracks: Bohemian Rhapsody • Boy Meets Girl • Bring Your Adz • Hallelujah • Pianoforte 2010 • Variation on a Dance 2010 • and more, plus two bonus selections!

00702516 . . . . $19.99

Rodgers & Hammerstein for Ukulele

arr. Jim Beloff

Now you can play 20 classic show tunes from this beloved songwriting duo on your uke! Includes: All at Once You Love Her • Do-Re-Mi • Edelweiss • Getting to Know You • Impossible • My Favorite Things • and more.

00701905 . . . . $12.99

HAL•LEONARD® CORPORATION

7777 W. BLUEMOUND RD. P.O. BOX 13819 MILWAUKEE, WI 53213

0212